50 Delicious Tapas for Any Occasion

By: Kelly Johnson

Table of Contents

- Patatas Bravas
- Gambas al Ajillo (Garlic Shrimp)
- Chorizo al Vino (Chorizo in Red Wine)
- Tortilla Española (Spanish Omelette)
- Pimientos de Padrón (Sauteed Padrón Peppers)
- Albondigas (Spanish Meatballs)
- Pan con Tomate (Tomato Toast)
- Croquetas de Jamón (Ham Croquettes)
- Calamares a la Romana (Fried Squid)
- Pulpo a la Gallega (Galician-Style Octopus)
- Queso Manchego with Membrillo
- Ensaladilla Rusa (Russian Salad)
- Banderillas (Pickled Skewers)
- Jamón Ibérico with Olives
- Tortilla de Patatas Mini
- Chistorra Sausage Bites
- Espinacas con Garbanzos (Spinach and Chickpeas)
- Tzatziki with Pita Bread
- Marinated Anchovies (Boquerones)
- Sautéed Mushrooms with Garlic and Parsley
- Frittata with Chard and Potatoes
- Patatas a la Riojana (Potatoes with Chorizo)
- Figs Stuffed with Blue Cheese and Wrapped in Prosciutto
- Empanadas de Carne (Meat Empanadas)
- Gambas al Pil Pil (Chili Garlic Shrimp)
- Bocadillos de Calamares (Squid Sandwiches)
- Pinchos Morunos (Moroccan-Spiced Skewers)
- Stuffed Piquillo Peppers with Tuna
- Ceviche with Lemon and Cilantro
- Grilled Vegetables with Romesco Sauce
- Manchego Cheese with Quince Paste
- Churros with Chocolate Sauce
- Piquillo Peppers Stuffed with Crab
- Spanish Anchovy and Tomato Salad
- Roasted Red Pepper and Garlic Dip

- Patatas Bravas with Aioli
- Gaspacho Andaluz (Cold Tomato Soup)
- Arroz Negro (Black Rice with Squid Ink)
- Tinto de Verano (Summer Red Wine Cocktail)
- Spanish Meat and Cheese Platter
- Spinach and Ricotta Empanadas
- Cured Salmon with Avocado and Lime
- Squid Ink Croquettes
- Jamón Serrano with Melon
- Goat Cheese Croquettes with Honey
- Spanish Sardines with Lemon
- Manchego and Fig Jam Crostini
- Octopus and Potato Salad
- Croquetas de Bacalao (Cod Croquettes)
- Grilled Lamb Chops with Mint Yogurt

Patatas Bravas

Ingredients:

- 4 medium potatoes, peeled and cubed
- 2 tbsp olive oil
- Salt, to taste
- 1/2 cup tomato sauce
- 1 tbsp smoked paprika
- 1 tbsp white wine vinegar
- 1/4 tsp cayenne pepper (optional)

Instructions:

1. **Prepare the potatoes**: Heat olive oil in a large frying pan over medium heat. Add the cubed potatoes and cook, stirring occasionally, until golden and crispy, about 10-15 minutes. Season with salt and set aside.
2. **Make the sauce**: In a small saucepan, heat tomato sauce, smoked paprika, white wine vinegar, and cayenne pepper over low heat. Stir to combine and cook for about 5 minutes.
3. **Serve**: Pour the sauce over the crispy potatoes or serve it on the side as a dipping sauce.

Gambas al Ajillo (Garlic Shrimp)

Ingredients:

- 1 lb shrimp, peeled and deveined
- 4 cloves garlic, thinly sliced
- 1/4 cup olive oil
- 1/4 tsp red pepper flakes
- Salt, to taste
- Fresh parsley, chopped (for garnish)
- Lemon wedges (for serving)

Instructions:

1. **Cook the garlic:** In a large skillet, heat olive oil over medium heat. Add sliced garlic and red pepper flakes and sauté until garlic becomes fragrant and golden brown, about 2 minutes.
2. **Cook the shrimp:** Add the shrimp to the skillet and cook for 2-3 minutes per side, or until they turn pink and opaque.
3. **Garnish and serve:** Season with salt, sprinkle with chopped parsley, and serve with lemon wedges.

Chorizo al Vino (Chorizo in Red Wine)

Ingredients:

- 1 lb Spanish chorizo, sliced
- 1 cup red wine
- 1/4 cup olive oil
- 2 cloves garlic, minced
- 1 tbsp fresh thyme or rosemary

Instructions:

1. **Brown the chorizo**: Heat olive oil in a large skillet over medium heat. Add the chorizo slices and cook until browned and crispy, about 5-7 minutes. Remove from the pan and set aside.
2. **Cook the wine**: In the same pan, add garlic and cook for 1-2 minutes until fragrant. Pour in the red wine and bring to a simmer, scraping up any bits from the bottom of the pan.
3. **Simmer**: Add the chorizo back to the pan and simmer for 5-7 minutes, allowing the flavors to meld and the wine to reduce slightly.
4. **Serve**: Sprinkle with fresh thyme or rosemary before serving.

Tortilla Española (Spanish Omelette)

Ingredients:

- 6 large eggs
- 3 medium potatoes, peeled and thinly sliced
- 1 onion, thinly sliced
- 1/4 cup olive oil
- Salt and pepper, to taste

Instructions:

1. **Cook the potatoes and onion**: Heat olive oil in a large skillet over medium heat. Add the potatoes and onion, season with salt and pepper, and cook until soft and slightly golden, about 10 minutes.
2. **Whisk the eggs**: In a bowl, whisk the eggs with salt and pepper. Add the cooked potatoes and onions to the eggs, stirring gently to combine.
3. **Cook the tortilla**: Heat a little olive oil in a non-stick skillet. Pour the egg-potato mixture into the skillet and cook over low heat, gently shaking the pan to prevent sticking. Cook for 8-10 minutes, then flip carefully (using a plate or lid) and cook for another 5-7 minutes, until fully set.
4. **Serve**: Let the tortilla cool for a few minutes before slicing and serving.

Pimientos de Padrón (Sauteed Padrón Peppers)

Ingredients:

- 1 lb Padrón peppers
- 2 tbsp olive oil
- Salt, to taste

Instructions:

1. **Cook the peppers**: Heat olive oil in a frying pan over medium-high heat. Add the Padrón peppers and sauté for 5-7 minutes, or until they are blistered and charred.
2. **Serve**: Season with sea salt and serve immediately as a snack or tapa.

Albondigas (Spanish Meatballs)

Ingredients:

- 1 lb ground beef
- 1/4 cup breadcrumbs
- 1 egg
- 2 cloves garlic, minced
- 1/4 cup parsley, chopped
- 1/4 cup onion, finely chopped
- Salt and pepper, to taste
- 1/2 cup tomato sauce
- 1/4 tsp smoked paprika

Instructions:

1. **Make the meatballs**: In a large bowl, combine ground beef, breadcrumbs, egg, garlic, parsley, onion, salt, and pepper. Mix well and form into small meatballs.
2. **Cook the meatballs**: Heat olive oil in a large skillet over medium heat. Brown the meatballs on all sides, about 8 minutes.
3. **Make the sauce**: In the same pan, add the tomato sauce and smoked paprika. Simmer the meatballs in the sauce for an additional 10 minutes, until cooked through.
4. **Serve**: Garnish with fresh parsley and serve warm.

Pan con Tomate (Tomato Toast)

Ingredients:

- 4 slices of rustic bread, toasted
- 2 ripe tomatoes, halved
- 2 cloves garlic, peeled
- Olive oil, for drizzling
- Salt and pepper, to taste

Instructions:

1. **Prepare the toast**: Toast the slices of rustic bread in a toaster or on a grill.
2. **Rub with garlic and tomato**: Rub each slice of toast with the peeled garlic cloves, then rub the cut side of the tomato onto the bread, extracting the juices and pulp.
3. **Finish and serve**: Drizzle with olive oil, sprinkle with salt and pepper, and serve immediately.

Croquetas de Jamón (Ham Croquettes)

Ingredients:

- 1 cup cooked ham, finely chopped
- 2 tbsp unsalted butter
- 1/4 cup all-purpose flour
- 1 cup whole milk
- 1/2 tsp nutmeg
- Salt and pepper, to taste
- 1/4 cup breadcrumbs
- 2 eggs, beaten
- Olive oil, for frying

Instructions:

1. **Make the filling**: In a skillet, melt butter over medium heat. Stir in the flour and cook for 1-2 minutes. Gradually add the milk, stirring constantly to avoid lumps. Cook until the mixture thickens, about 5 minutes. Stir in the ham, nutmeg, salt, and pepper, and cook for another 2 minutes.
2. **Shape the croquettes**: Allow the mixture to cool. Once cool, shape the mixture into small cylinders.
3. **Coat and fry**: Dip each croquette into the beaten eggs, then roll in breadcrumbs. Heat olive oil in a frying pan and fry the croquettes in batches until golden brown, about 3-4 minutes.
4. **Serve**: Drain on paper towels and serve hot.

Calamares a la Romana (Fried Squid)

Ingredients:

- 1 lb squid, cleaned and cut into rings
- 1 cup all-purpose flour
- 1 tsp paprika
- Salt and pepper to taste
- 1 egg, beaten
- Olive oil for frying
- Lemon wedges for serving

Instructions:

1. **Prepare the squid:**
   Rinse and dry the squid rings thoroughly with paper towels.
2. **Season the flour:**
   In a shallow bowl, mix the flour, paprika, salt, and pepper.
3. **Coat the squid:**
   Dip each squid ring first into the beaten egg, then coat it in the seasoned flour.
4. **Fry the squid:**
   Heat olive oil in a frying pan over medium-high heat. Fry the squid in batches for 2-3 minutes, or until golden and crispy.
5. **Drain and serve:**
   Remove the squid from the oil and drain on paper towels. Serve hot with lemon wedges.

Pulpo a la Gallega (Galician-Style Octopus)

Ingredients:

- 1 lb octopus, cleaned and tentacles cut into rings
- 2 medium potatoes, peeled and sliced
- 1/4 cup olive oil
- 1 tsp smoked paprika
- Salt to taste
- Fresh parsley for garnish (optional)

Instructions:

1. **Cook the octopus:**
   Bring a large pot of water to a boil and add the octopus. Simmer for 40-45 minutes, or until the octopus is tender.
2. **Cook the potatoes:**
   While the octopus cooks, boil the potato slices in a separate pot of water until tender, about 10-15 minutes.
3. **Prepare the dish:**
   Arrange the boiled potatoes on a serving plate. Place the octopus slices on top.
4. **Season and serve:**
   Drizzle with olive oil, sprinkle with smoked paprika, and season with salt. Garnish with parsley if desired. Serve warm.

Queso Manchego with Membrillo

Ingredients:

- 8 oz Queso Manchego cheese, sliced
- 1/2 cup membrillo (quince paste)
- Fresh bread or crackers for serving

Instructions:

1. **Slice the cheese:**
   Slice the Queso Manchego into thin wedges or cubes.
2. **Serve:**
   Arrange the cheese on a serving platter and serve with slices of membrillo (quince paste) and fresh bread or crackers.

Ensaladilla Rusa (Russian Salad)

Ingredients:

- 3 medium potatoes, peeled and diced
- 1 cup frozen peas
- 1/2 cup carrots, diced
- 1/2 cup mayonnaise
- 1/4 cup olive oil
- Salt and pepper to taste
- 2 hard-boiled eggs, chopped (optional)
- Pimentos for garnish (optional)

Instructions:

1. **Cook the vegetables**:
   Boil the potatoes and carrots in a large pot until tender. Add the peas during the last 5 minutes of cooking. Drain and let cool.
2. **Mix the salad**:
   In a large bowl, combine the potatoes, carrots, peas, and hard-boiled eggs (if using). Stir in the mayonnaise and olive oil. Season with salt and pepper.
3. **Serve**:
   Transfer to a serving dish and garnish with pimentos. Chill in the refrigerator before serving.

Banderillas (Pickled Skewers)

Ingredients:

- 10 small pickled gherkin cucumbers
- 10 small pickled onions
- 10 green olives
- 10 slices of Spanish chorizo
- 10 cocktail sticks

Instructions:

1. **Assemble the skewers**:
   On each cocktail stick, alternate threading a gherkin cucumber, pickled onion, green olive, and slice of chorizo.
2. **Serve**:
   Arrange the banderillas on a platter and serve immediately as a tapas dish.

Jamón Ibérico with Olives

Ingredients:

- 4 oz Jamón Ibérico, thinly sliced
- 1/2 cup green olives
- 1/2 cup black olives

Instructions:

1. **Prepare the plate:**
   Arrange the thin slices of Jamón Ibérico on a platter.
2. **Add olives:**
   Place the green and black olives on the plate alongside the ham.
3. **Serve:**
   Serve immediately as a simple and delicious tapas dish.

Tortilla de Patatas Mini

Ingredients:

- 4 medium potatoes, peeled and diced
- 1 small onion, finely chopped
- 4 large eggs, beaten
- Olive oil for frying
- Salt to taste

Instructions:

1. **Cook the potatoes and onions:**
   Heat olive oil in a frying pan over medium heat. Add the potatoes and onions, cooking until the potatoes are soft and golden.
2. **Mix with eggs:**
   Drain the potatoes and onions on paper towels to remove excess oil. Let cool slightly. In a bowl, combine the potatoes, onions, and beaten eggs. Season with salt.
3. **Cook the tortilla:**
   Heat a small amount of olive oil in the pan and pour in the egg mixture. Cook over low heat until the edges are set and golden. Flip the tortilla and cook for another 2-3 minutes until fully cooked through.
4. **Serve:**
   Let cool slightly and cut into mini wedges to serve.

Chistorra Sausage Bites

Ingredients:

- 1 lb chistorra sausages
- Toothpicks for serving

Instructions:

1. **Cook the chistorra**:
   Heat a skillet over medium heat. Cook the chistorra sausages, turning occasionally, until they are fully cooked and browned on all sides.
2. **Slice the sausages**:
   Remove the sausages from the skillet and let cool slightly. Cut them into bite-sized pieces.
3. **Serve**:
   Arrange the sausage pieces on a platter and serve with toothpicks for easy eating.

Espinacas con Garbanzos (Spinach and Chickpeas)

Ingredients:

- 2 cups fresh spinach, washed and chopped
- 1 can (15 oz) chickpeas, drained and rinsed
- 2 cloves garlic, minced
- 1 tsp cumin
- 1/2 tsp paprika
- Olive oil
- Salt and pepper to taste
- A pinch of cayenne pepper (optional)
- Lemon wedges for serving

Instructions:

1. **Cook the chickpeas**:
   In a large skillet, heat a tablespoon of olive oil over medium heat. Add the chickpeas and sauté for 2-3 minutes until slightly crispy. Remove from the skillet and set aside.
2. **Sauté the spinach**:
   In the same skillet, add a bit more olive oil and sauté the garlic over medium heat for about 1 minute until fragrant. Add the chopped spinach and cook until wilted.
3. **Combine**:
   Stir in the cumin, paprika, cayenne (if using), and the cooked chickpeas. Cook for another 2-3 minutes, allowing the flavors to meld together.
4. **Serve**:
   Season with salt and pepper to taste, then serve hot with lemon wedges on the side.

Tzatziki with Pita Bread

Ingredients:

- 1 cup Greek yogurt
- 1 cucumber, grated and excess water squeezed out
- 2 cloves garlic, minced
- 1 tbsp olive oil
- 1 tbsp fresh lemon juice
- 1 tbsp fresh dill, chopped
- Salt and pepper to taste
- Pita bread, cut into wedges

Instructions:

1. **Prepare the tzatziki:**
   In a bowl, combine the yogurt, grated cucumber, garlic, olive oil, lemon juice, and dill. Stir well until smooth.
2. **Season:**
   Add salt and pepper to taste. Let the tzatziki sit in the fridge for at least 30 minutes to allow the flavors to blend.
3. **Serve:**
   Serve the tzatziki chilled with warm pita bread wedges for dipping.

Marinated Anchovies (Boquerones)

Ingredients:

- 1 lb fresh anchovies, cleaned and filleted
- 1/2 cup white wine vinegar
- 1/2 cup olive oil
- 2 cloves garlic, sliced
- 1/4 cup fresh parsley, chopped
- Salt to taste

Instructions:

1. **Prepare the anchovies**:
   Place the anchovy fillets in a shallow dish. Pour the vinegar over them and let them marinate for 1 hour in the refrigerator.
2. **Marinate**:
   After 1 hour, drain the anchovies and arrange them on a plate. Drizzle with olive oil, top with sliced garlic and chopped parsley, and season with salt.
3. **Serve**:
   Let the anchovies marinate for another 30 minutes before serving as a cold tapas dish.

Sautéed Mushrooms with Garlic and Parsley

Ingredients:

- 1 lb mushrooms, sliced
- 3 cloves garlic, minced
- 2 tbsp olive oil
- 1/4 cup fresh parsley, chopped
- Salt and pepper to taste

Instructions:

1. **Sauté the mushrooms:**
   Heat olive oil in a large skillet over medium heat. Add the mushrooms and sauté for 5-7 minutes until golden and tender.
2. **Add garlic and parsley:**
   Add the minced garlic to the pan and sauté for another minute until fragrant. Stir in the fresh parsley.
3. **Season:**
   Season with salt and pepper to taste and serve warm.

Frittata with Chard and Potatoes

Ingredients:

- 6 large eggs, beaten
- 2 cups Swiss chard, chopped
- 2 medium potatoes, peeled and thinly sliced
- 1 small onion, finely chopped
- Olive oil
- Salt and pepper to taste

Instructions:

1. **Prepare the potatoes:**
   Heat olive oil in a large oven-safe skillet over medium heat. Add the potatoes and cook until soft and golden, about 10 minutes. Remove the potatoes and set aside.
2. **Cook the chard and onions:**
   In the same skillet, sauté the onions in olive oil until soft. Add the chopped Swiss chard and cook until wilted.
3. **Make the frittata:**
   Add the cooked potatoes back to the skillet, pour the beaten eggs over the vegetables, and season with salt and pepper. Cook over low heat for 5 minutes, then transfer to a preheated oven at 350°F for 10-12 minutes until set.
4. **Serve:**
   Let the frittata cool slightly, slice into wedges, and serve warm.

Patatas a la Riojana (Potatoes with Chorizo)

Ingredients:

- 2 large potatoes, peeled and diced
- 1/2 lb chorizo sausage, sliced
- 1 onion, chopped
- 2 cloves garlic, minced
- 1 tsp paprika
- 4 cups chicken broth
- Olive oil
- Salt to taste

Instructions:

1. **Cook the chorizo:**
   Heat olive oil in a large pot over medium heat. Add the sliced chorizo and cook until browned, about 5 minutes. Remove and set aside.
2. **Cook the vegetables:**
   In the same pot, sauté the onion and garlic until softened. Add the diced potatoes and paprika, and stir well to combine.
3. **Simmer:**
   Add the chicken broth and bring to a boil. Reduce the heat and simmer for 20 minutes, or until the potatoes are tender. Add the cooked chorizo back into the pot and simmer for another 5 minutes.
4. **Serve:**
   Season with salt and serve warm.

Figs Stuffed with Blue Cheese and Wrapped in Prosciutto

Ingredients:

- 12 fresh figs, halved
- 4 oz blue cheese, crumbled
- 6 slices prosciutto, cut in half
- Honey for drizzling (optional)

Instructions:

1. **Prepare the figs**:
   Cut the figs in half and remove the stems.
2. **Stuff with cheese**:
   Place a small amount of blue cheese in the center of each fig half.
3. **Wrap with prosciutto**:
   Wrap each stuffed fig with a slice of prosciutto and secure with a toothpick.
4. **Serve**:
   Arrange the figs on a platter and drizzle with honey if desired. Serve immediately.

Empanadas de Carne (Meat Empanadas)

Ingredients:

- 1 lb ground beef
- 1 small onion, finely chopped
- 1/2 cup green olives, chopped
- 1/4 cup raisins
- 1 tsp cumin
- 1/2 tsp paprika
- 1 package empanada dough discs
- Olive oil for frying
- Salt and pepper to taste

Instructions:

1. **Cook the filling**:
   In a skillet, cook the ground beef and onion over medium heat until browned. Stir in the olives, raisins, cumin, paprika, salt, and pepper. Cook for 2-3 minutes, then let the mixture cool.
2. **Assemble the empanadas**:
   Place a spoonful of the meat mixture in the center of each empanada dough disc. Fold the dough over to form a half-moon shape and seal the edges by crimping with a fork.
3. **Fry the empanadas**:
   Heat olive oil in a frying pan over medium heat. Fry the empanadas in batches for 3-4 minutes per side, or until golden brown.
4. **Serve**:
   Drain on paper towels and serve hot.

Gambas al Pil Pil (Chili Garlic Shrimp)

Ingredients:

- 1 lb large shrimp, peeled and deveined
- 4 cloves garlic, sliced
- 1-2 dried red chilies
- 1/4 cup olive oil
- Salt and pepper to taste
- Fresh parsley, chopped

Instructions:

1. **Cook the garlic and chilies:**
   Heat olive oil in a large skillet over medium heat. Add the garlic and dried chilies, and sauté for 1-2 minutes until fragrant.
2. **Cook the shrimp:**
   Add the shrimp to the skillet and cook for 3-4 minutes, or until pink and opaque.
3. **Serve:**
   Season with salt and pepper, sprinkle with chopped parsley, and serve hot with crusty bread for dipping.

Bocadillos de Calamares (Squid Sandwiches)

Ingredients:

- 1 lb squid, cleaned and cut into rings
- 1 cup all-purpose flour
- 1 tsp paprika
- Salt and pepper to taste
- Olive oil for frying
- 4 small baguettes or sandwich rolls
- Lemon wedges
- Fresh parsley, chopped

Instructions:

1. **Prepare the squid**:
   Rinse and pat the squid rings dry with paper towels. In a bowl, mix the flour, paprika, salt, and pepper.
2. **Fry the squid**:
   Heat olive oil in a deep pan over medium-high heat. Dredge the squid rings in the seasoned flour and fry them in batches for 2-3 minutes, or until golden and crispy. Remove and drain on paper towels.
3. **Assemble the bocadillos**:
   Slice the baguettes or rolls in half and lightly toast them. Fill each sandwich with the fried squid rings, and top with fresh parsley and a squeeze of lemon.
4. **Serve**:
   Serve the sandwiches hot, with extra lemon wedges on the side.

Pinchos Morunos (Moroccan-Spiced Skewers)

Ingredients:

- 1 lb pork tenderloin or chicken breast, cut into cubes
- 2 tbsp olive oil
- 1 tsp ground cumin
- 1 tsp ground coriander
- 1 tsp smoked paprika
- 1/2 tsp ground cinnamon
- 1/2 tsp ground turmeric
- 2 cloves garlic, minced
- 1 tbsp fresh lemon juice
- Salt and pepper to taste
- Fresh cilantro for garnish

Instructions:

1. **Marinate the meat**:
   In a bowl, combine the olive oil, cumin, coriander, paprika, cinnamon, turmeric, garlic, lemon juice, salt, and pepper. Add the meat cubes and toss to coat. Cover and marinate for at least 1 hour (or overnight for more flavor).
2. **Skewer the meat**:
   Thread the marinated meat onto skewers.
3. **Grill the pinchos**:
   Preheat the grill or a grill pan over medium-high heat. Grill the skewers for 4-5 minutes on each side, or until the meat is cooked through and lightly charred.
4. **Serve**:
   Garnish with fresh cilantro and serve hot.

Stuffed Piquillo Peppers with Tuna

Ingredients:

- 12 piquillo peppers, drained and patted dry
- 1 can (5 oz) tuna in olive oil, drained and flaked
- 1/4 cup mayonnaise
- 1 tbsp Dijon mustard
- 1 tbsp fresh lemon juice
- 1 tbsp fresh parsley, chopped
- Salt and pepper to taste

Instructions:

1. **Prepare the filling:**
   In a bowl, combine the tuna, mayonnaise, Dijon mustard, lemon juice, parsley, salt, and pepper. Mix until smooth.
2. **Stuff the peppers:**
   Carefully stuff each piquillo pepper with the tuna mixture.
3. **Serve:**
   Arrange the stuffed peppers on a platter and serve cold or at room temperature.

Ceviche with Lemon and Cilantro

Ingredients:

- 1 lb fresh white fish (like cod or tilapia), diced
- 1/2 cup fresh lemon juice
- 1 small red onion, finely diced
- 1/2 cup fresh cilantro, chopped
- 1 small cucumber, peeled and diced
- 1 fresh chili, finely chopped (optional)
- Salt and pepper to taste

Instructions:

1. **Marinate the fish**:
   In a bowl, combine the diced fish with the lemon juice, and season with salt and pepper. Cover and refrigerate for 1-2 hours, or until the fish is opaque and "cooked" by the acid.
2. **Prepare the other ingredients**:
   While the fish is marinating, prepare the onion, cilantro, cucumber, and chili.
3. **Mix the ceviche**:
   After the fish has marinated, add the onion, cilantro, cucumber, and chili to the bowl. Stir gently to combine.
4. **Serve**:
   Serve chilled in small cups or bowls, garnished with extra cilantro.

Grilled Vegetables with Romesco Sauce

Ingredients:

- 1 red bell pepper, cut into quarters
- 1 yellow bell pepper, cut into quarters
- 1 zucchini, sliced
- 1 eggplant, sliced
- Olive oil
- Salt and pepper to taste

For the Romesco Sauce:

- 1/2 cup roasted red peppers (jarred)
- 1/4 cup almonds, toasted
- 1/4 cup olive oil
- 1 tbsp red wine vinegar
- 1 garlic clove
- 1 tsp smoked paprika
- Salt and pepper to taste

Instructions:

1. **Grill the vegetables:**
   Preheat the grill to medium-high heat. Drizzle the vegetables with olive oil, season with salt and pepper, and grill for 4-5 minutes per side, or until tender and lightly charred.
2. **Make the romesco sauce:**
   In a food processor, combine the roasted red peppers, toasted almonds, olive oil, vinegar, garlic, paprika, salt, and pepper. Blend until smooth.
3. **Serve:**
   Arrange the grilled vegetables on a platter and drizzle with the romesco sauce. Serve warm or at room temperature.

Manchego Cheese with Quince Paste

Ingredients:

- 8 oz Manchego cheese, sliced
- 1/4 cup quince paste (membrillo), sliced

Instructions:

1. **Prepare the cheese and quince**:
   Slice the Manchego cheese and quince paste into thin pieces.
2. **Serve**:
   Arrange the cheese and quince paste slices on a platter and serve as an appetizer or tapas dish.

Churros with Chocolate Sauce

Ingredients:

For the churros:

- 1 cup water
- 2 tbsp butter
- 1/4 tsp salt
- 1 cup all-purpose flour
- 2 eggs
- 1 tbsp sugar
- Oil for frying

For the chocolate sauce:

- 4 oz dark chocolate, chopped
- 1/2 cup heavy cream
- 1 tbsp sugar

Instructions:

1. **Make the churros dough:**
   In a saucepan, bring water, butter, and salt to a boil. Stir in the flour and cook, stirring constantly, until the dough forms a ball. Remove from heat and let cool slightly. Beat in the eggs, one at a time, until smooth.
2. **Fry the churros:**
   Heat oil in a deep fryer or pot to 350°F. Spoon the churros dough into a piping bag with a star tip. Pipe the dough into the hot oil, cutting it into 4-inch lengths. Fry until golden brown, about 3-4 minutes. Drain on paper towels and sprinkle with sugar.
3. **Make the chocolate sauce:**
   In a small saucepan, heat the heavy cream until simmering. Remove from heat and stir in the chopped chocolate and sugar until smooth.
4. **Serve:**
   Serve the churros warm, with the chocolate sauce on the side for dipping.

Piquillo Peppers Stuffed with Crab

Ingredients:

- 12 piquillo peppers, drained and patted dry
- 1/2 lb fresh crab meat (or imitation crab)
- 1/4 cup mayonnaise
- 1 tbsp Dijon mustard
- 1 tbsp fresh lemon juice
- 2 tbsp fresh parsley, chopped
- Salt and pepper to taste

Instructions:

1. **Prepare the crab filling:**
   In a bowl, combine the crab meat, mayonnaise, Dijon mustard, lemon juice, parsley, salt, and pepper. Stir gently to combine.
2. **Stuff the peppers:**
   Carefully stuff each piquillo pepper with the crab mixture.
3. **Serve:**
   Arrange the stuffed peppers on a platter and serve cold or at room temperature.

Spanish Anchovy and Tomato Salad

Ingredients:

- 1 can (4 oz) anchovy fillets, drained
- 2 ripe tomatoes, sliced
- 1 small red onion, thinly sliced
- 1/4 cup green olives, pitted and halved
- 2 tbsp extra virgin olive oil
- 1 tbsp red wine vinegar
- 1 tsp dried oregano
- Salt and pepper to taste
- Fresh parsley, chopped (for garnish)

Instructions:

1. **Prepare the salad:**
   In a large bowl, combine the sliced tomatoes, onion, olives, and anchovy fillets.
2. **Make the dressing:**
   In a small bowl, whisk together the olive oil, red wine vinegar, oregano, salt, and pepper.
3. **Toss the salad:**
   Drizzle the dressing over the tomato mixture and toss gently to combine.
4. **Serve:**
   Garnish with fresh parsley and serve chilled or at room temperature.

Roasted Red Pepper and Garlic Dip

Ingredients:

- 2 red bell peppers, roasted, peeled, and seeded
- 2 garlic cloves, roasted
- 1/4 cup olive oil
- 1 tbsp red wine vinegar
- 1/2 tsp smoked paprika
- Salt and pepper to taste

Instructions:

1. **Prepare the peppers and garlic:**
   Roast the red peppers under the broiler or on a grill until the skins are charred. Place them in a bowl, cover with plastic wrap, and let them steam for 10 minutes. Peel off the skins, remove the seeds, and set aside. Roast the garlic in foil for 15 minutes until soft.
2. **Make the dip:**
   In a food processor, combine the roasted peppers, garlic, olive oil, red wine vinegar, smoked paprika, salt, and pepper. Blend until smooth.
3. **Serve:**
   Serve the dip with crusty bread, crackers, or raw vegetables.

Patatas Bravas with Aioli

Ingredients:

For the Patatas Bravas:

- 4 medium potatoes, peeled and cut into cubes
- Olive oil for frying
- Salt and pepper to taste

For the Brava Sauce:

- 1/4 cup olive oil
- 1 small onion, finely chopped
- 2 garlic cloves, minced
- 1 tsp smoked paprika
- 1/2 tsp cayenne pepper
- 1 can (14 oz) crushed tomatoes
- 1 tbsp red wine vinegar
- Salt and pepper to taste

For the Aioli:

- 1/2 cup mayonnaise
- 1 tbsp garlic, minced
- 1 tbsp lemon juice
- Salt to taste

Instructions:

1. **Prepare the Brava Sauce:**
   In a pan, heat olive oil over medium heat. Add the onion and garlic, and cook until softened. Stir in the paprika and cayenne, and cook for another minute. Add the crushed tomatoes and vinegar, and simmer for 15 minutes. Season with salt and pepper.
2. **Make the aioli:**
   In a small bowl, mix together the mayonnaise, garlic, lemon juice, and salt.
3. **Fry the potatoes:**
   Heat olive oil in a large pan over medium-high heat. Fry the potato cubes until golden and crispy, about 10 minutes. Drain on paper towels and season with salt.

4. **Serve**:
    Serve the fried potatoes with the brava sauce and aioli on the side.

Gazpacho Andaluz (Cold Tomato Soup)

Ingredients:

- 6 ripe tomatoes, peeled and chopped
- 1 cucumber, peeled and chopped
- 1 red bell pepper, chopped
- 1/2 red onion, chopped
- 2 garlic cloves
- 1/4 cup extra virgin olive oil
- 2 tbsp red wine vinegar
- 2 cups tomato juice
- Salt and pepper to taste
- Fresh basil or parsley for garnish

Instructions:

1. **Blend the ingredients**:
   In a blender or food processor, combine the tomatoes, cucumber, bell pepper, onion, garlic, olive oil, red wine vinegar, and tomato juice. Blend until smooth.
2. **Chill**:
   Refrigerate the gazpacho for at least 2 hours before serving.
3. **Serve**:
   Serve chilled in bowls, garnished with fresh basil or parsley.

Arroz Negro (Black Rice with Squid Ink)

Ingredients:

- 1 lb squid, cleaned and cut into rings
- 2 cups short-grain rice (like Arborio)
- 1/4 cup olive oil
- 1 small onion, finely chopped
- 2 garlic cloves, minced
- 1 red bell pepper, chopped
- 1/2 cup white wine
- 4 cups fish or vegetable broth
- 2 tbsp squid ink
- Salt and pepper to taste
- Lemon wedges for serving

Instructions:

1. **Cook the squid**:
   Heat olive oil in a large pan over medium-high heat. Add the squid rings and cook for 3-4 minutes until they release their juices and begin to brown. Remove and set aside.
2. **Prepare the rice**:
   In the same pan, add the onion, garlic, and bell pepper. Cook until softened, about 5 minutes. Stir in the rice and cook for 2 minutes, allowing it to lightly toast. Add the white wine and cook for 1 minute.
3. **Simmer the rice**:
   Add the broth and bring to a simmer. Cover and cook for 15-20 minutes, until the rice is tender and the liquid is absorbed. Stir in the squid ink, salt, and pepper.
4. **Serve**:
   Stir the cooked squid back into the rice. Serve hot, with lemon wedges on the side.

Tinto de Verano (Summer Red Wine Cocktail)

Ingredients:

- 1 cup red wine (Spanish Tempranillo works best)
- 1/2 cup lemon soda (like Sprite or a lemon-lime soda)
- Ice
- Lemon slices for garnish

Instructions:

1. **Prepare the cocktail**:
   In a glass, combine the red wine and lemon soda over ice.
2. **Serve**:
   Garnish with lemon slices and serve chilled.

Spanish Meat and Cheese Platter

Ingredients:

- 1/2 lb cured Spanish meats (chorizo, jamón ibérico, salchichón)
- 1/2 lb Spanish cheeses (Manchego, Cabrales, Mahón)
- Green olives
- Marinated artichokes
- Fresh bread or crackers

Instructions:

1. **Arrange the platter:**
   On a large serving platter, arrange the meats and cheeses in an attractive way. Add olives, artichokes, and fresh bread or crackers.
2. **Serve:**
   Serve as an appetizer or tapas for a gathering.

Spinach and Ricotta Empanadas

Ingredients:

- 1 package empanada dough discs
- 1 cup fresh spinach, chopped
- 1/2 cup ricotta cheese
- 1/4 cup grated Parmesan cheese
- 1 egg, beaten (for sealing)
- Olive oil for brushing

Instructions:

1. **Prepare the filling**:
   In a skillet, heat a little olive oil and sauté the spinach until wilted. Remove from heat and let it cool. In a bowl, mix the spinach, ricotta, and Parmesan cheese.
2. **Assemble the empanadas**:
   Place a spoonful of the spinach mixture in the center of each empanada dough disc. Brush the edges with the beaten egg and fold the dough over to form a half-moon shape. Seal the edges by pressing with a fork.
3. **Bake**:
   Preheat the oven to 375°F (190°C). Place the empanadas on a baking sheet lined with parchment paper. Brush the tops with olive oil and bake for 20-25 minutes, or until golden brown.
4. **Serve**:
   Serve warm as a snack or appetizer.

Cured Salmon with Avocado and Lime

Ingredients:

- 1 lb cured salmon (like gravlax or smoked salmon)
- 2 ripe avocados, sliced
- 1 lime, juiced
- Fresh dill, chopped (for garnish)
- Salt and pepper to taste

Instructions:

1. **Prepare the salmon and avocado:**
   Arrange the cured salmon on a platter. Layer the avocado slices next to the salmon.
2. **Season and garnish:**
   Drizzle the lime juice over the salmon and avocado. Sprinkle with salt, pepper, and fresh dill.
3. **Serve:**
   Serve immediately as a refreshing appetizer or light main course.

Squid Ink Croquettes

Ingredients:

- 1/2 lb squid, chopped
- 1/4 cup olive oil
- 1 small onion, finely chopped
- 2 garlic cloves, minced
- 1/2 cup squid ink
- 1/2 cup milk
- 1 1/2 cups breadcrumbs
- 1/2 cup flour
- 2 eggs, beaten
- Salt and pepper to taste
- Olive oil for frying

Instructions:

1. **Prepare the filling:**
   Heat olive oil in a pan and sauté the onion and garlic until softened. Add the chopped squid and cook until just tender. Stir in the squid ink and milk, and cook until the mixture thickens. Season with salt and pepper.
2. **Make the croquette mixture:**
   Transfer the squid mixture to a bowl and let it cool. Once cool, add breadcrumbs and mix until a firm dough forms. Shape the mixture into small oval croquettes.
3. **Coat the croquettes:**
   Dip each croquette into flour, then beaten eggs, and finally breadcrumbs.
4. **Fry the croquettes:**
   Heat oil in a pan over medium heat and fry the croquettes until golden brown on all sides.
5. **Serve:**
   Serve warm with a side of aioli or dipping sauce.

Jamón Serrano with Melon

Ingredients:

- 1/2 lb Jamón Serrano, thinly sliced
- 1 small melon (such as cantaloupe), cut into wedges

Instructions:

1. **Prepare the dish:**
   Arrange the melon wedges on a platter. Drape the thin slices of Jamón Serrano over the melon.
2. **Serve:**
   Serve immediately as a simple, refreshing appetizer. The saltiness of the jamón pairs beautifully with the sweet melon.

Goat Cheese Croquettes with Honey

Ingredients:

- 1/2 lb goat cheese, crumbled
- 1/2 cup flour
- 2 eggs, beaten
- 1 cup breadcrumbs
- 2 tbsp honey
- Olive oil for frying
- Salt and pepper to taste

Instructions:

1. **Prepare the croquette mixture:**
   In a bowl, mix the goat cheese with a pinch of salt and pepper. Shape the mixture into small croquettes.
2. **Coat the croquettes:**
   Dip each croquette into flour, then beaten eggs, and finally breadcrumbs.
3. **Fry the croquettes:**
   Heat oil in a pan and fry the croquettes until golden brown and crispy.
4. **Drizzle with honey:**
   Drizzle honey over the hot croquettes and serve.
5. **Serve:**
   Serve warm as an appetizer or snack.

Spanish Sardines with Lemon

Ingredients:

- 1 can (4 oz) Spanish sardines in olive oil
- 1 lemon, sliced
- Fresh parsley, chopped (for garnish)
- Salt and pepper to taste

Instructions:

1. **Prepare the sardines**:
   Open the can of sardines and drain the excess olive oil. Place the sardines on a serving platter.
2. **Season and garnish**:
   Drizzle the sardines with a little of the olive oil from the can. Season with salt and pepper, and top with fresh lemon slices and parsley.
3. **Serve**:
   Serve chilled or at room temperature as a quick snack or appetizer.

Manchego and Fig Jam Crostini

Ingredients:

- 1 loaf baguette, sliced into 1/2-inch rounds
- 1/2 lb Manchego cheese, thinly sliced
- 1/4 cup fig jam
- Olive oil for brushing

Instructions:

1. **Prepare the crostini:**
   Preheat the oven to 375°F (190°C). Brush the baguette slices with olive oil and place them on a baking sheet. Toast in the oven for 5-7 minutes, or until golden brown.
2. **Assemble the crostini:**
   Spread a thin layer of fig jam on each toasted baguette slice. Top with a slice of Manchego cheese.
3. **Serve:**
   Serve as a savory-sweet appetizer at room temperature.

Octopus and Potato Salad

Ingredients:

- 1 lb octopus, cleaned and cooked
- 4 medium potatoes, boiled and diced
- 1/4 cup extra virgin olive oil
- 2 tbsp red wine vinegar
- 1 tbsp fresh lemon juice
- 1 small red onion, finely chopped
- 2 tbsp fresh parsley, chopped
- Salt and pepper to taste

Instructions:

1. **Prepare the octopus**:
   Cook the octopus in boiling water for about 40-45 minutes, until tender. Once cooled, cut the octopus into bite-sized pieces.
2. **Assemble the salad**:
   In a large bowl, combine the diced potatoes, octopus, onion, and parsley.
3. **Dress the salad**:
   In a small bowl, whisk together the olive oil, vinegar, lemon juice, salt, and pepper. Pour the dressing over the salad and toss gently to combine.
4. **Serve**:
   Serve immediately or refrigerate for an hour to allow the flavors to meld.

Croquetas de Bacalao (Cod Croquettes)

Ingredients:

- 1 lb salt cod, soaked and flaked
- 1 small onion, finely chopped
- 2 tbsp olive oil
- 1/2 cup flour
- 1 cup milk
- 2 eggs, beaten
- 1 1/2 cups breadcrumbs
- Salt and pepper to taste
- Olive oil for frying

Instructions:

1. **Prepare the cod filling**:
   Heat olive oil in a pan and sauté the onion until softened. Add the flaked cod and cook for a few minutes. Stir in flour and cook for 1-2 minutes, then slowly add the milk, stirring constantly to create a thick paste. Season with salt and pepper.
2. **Shape the croquettes**:
   Once the mixture cools, shape it into small croquettes.
3. **Coat the croquettes**:
   Dip each croquette into beaten egg and breadcrumbs.
4. **Fry the croquettes**:
   Heat oil in a pan and fry the croquettes until golden and crispy.
5. **Serve**:
   Serve warm with a side of aioli for dipping.

Grilled Lamb Chops with Mint Yogurt

Ingredients:

- 8 lamb chops
- 2 tbsp olive oil
- 1 tbsp fresh rosemary, chopped
- 1 tbsp garlic, minced
- Salt and pepper to taste
- 1/2 cup Greek yogurt
- 2 tbsp fresh mint, chopped
- 1 tbsp lemon juice

Instructions:

1. **Marinate the lamb chops**:
   In a bowl, combine olive oil, rosemary, garlic, salt, and pepper. Coat the lamb chops with the marinade and refrigerate for at least 1 hour.
2. **Grill the lamb**:
   Preheat the grill to medium-high heat. Grill the lamb chops for 4-5 minutes per side, or until desired doneness.
3. **Prepare the mint yogurt**:
   In a bowl, mix the Greek yogurt, fresh mint, and lemon juice. Season with salt to taste.
4. **Serve**:
   Serve the grilled lamb chops with a dollop of mint yogurt on the side.